Indy Joe

An Independent Voter Speaks

Table of Contents

Introduction

Our political system is dysfunctional and failing the average person. I feel frustrated and want to voice my opinions, but I am fearful of retaliation. Today, your political views can cause you to lose your job, become the victim of bullying, or suffer worse consequences. Is this the sign that our democracy is eroding? The highly charged environment of "I'm right, and you're wrong", does not allow for an informed and respectful discussion about current issues. Truth and facts are pushed aside by sensationalized news and Internet screaming amplified by selective hearing syndrome: a disorder that allows only affirming arguments to be heard. A counterargument grounded in confirming facts, will be disregarded if it does not support the person's predetermined opinion.

On social media, we see an abundance of people who act like experts in subjects about which they lack understanding. Their opinions are uninformed and without substance. Still, these self-proclaimed authorities conclude they have "common-sense", which trumps expert and scientific knowledge. Anti-vaxxers, climate change deniers, those who refute man landed on the moon, or people who reject that smoking causes cancer, all claim to have super-intelligence. They assert the experts and scientists are lying. Often, these self-appointed authorities are the loudest people in a conversation, becoming accusatory when someone disagrees with their point of view.

As an Independent voter, I feel my views are not being heard. Today's toxic political environment causes me to withdraw from the conversation. But given my frustration with our elected officials, not speaking out would also be wrong. I am not a politician, nor a student of politics, or connected to politics in any way. I am just a tax-paying citizen who is dismayed at the direction of our country. Therefore, I felt it necessary to express my views by writing this treatise.

The fact that you are reading this indicates you want to hear my opinion without the chatter. Thank you for taking the time to do so.

Indy Joe

I do not identify as either a Republican or a Democrat. I identify as an American. I have a family. I work hard. I am highly stressed. I earn just enough to pay the bills. At the same time, more and more financial burden is being placed on my family in the form of education, health care, and the cost of everyday goods. Uncertainty of a stable future is pushing retirement further away. The goal of living a low-stress, fun-filled old age is a dream I feel will never be fulfilled. I am not happy. Something is wrong.

Daily I am concerned for the safety of my family. Gun violence has become commonplace in our country. Will my family be able to go shopping without becoming a shooting statistic? Will I be the target of road rage or some other senseless violence? Are my children targets of the next wacko when they go to school? These are questions that I never thought of a few years ago. Now they are a real consideration.

What happened to the days when people respected each other; when they said "please" and "thank you"; and when genuine kindness was the norm? There is the feeling that everyone in our country is on-edge all the time.

The stress of living increases daily. It is as though my family and I are paying the debt for someone else's ideology, both financially and physically.

When I look at Washington, and our elected officials, I see people in top places who don't care about my problems. Even though I feel they play a significant role in making "my problems" - my problems. So who is to blame? Well, to be truthful, I am and you are. We, the voters, need to shoulder the blame because we elected these very same politicians. You can make a technical argument about gerrymandering and other maneuvers regarding voter restrictions. But the bottom line is these voter constraints would not be abused if the people that you and I voted into office were honest, had integrity, and considered the American people when making decisions.

Don't misunderstand me. I do not believe all politicians are trying to make my life a living hell. In fact, I think most are trying to do their job in the best interest of the people and the country. But it only takes a few elected officials in the right places to hijack our democracy.

Our government is a hybrid of a democracy and a republic. That is, voters elect representatives who have the responsibility to enact legislation desired by their constituents. In essence, the requirements of the people and the Constitution should be the guide for lawmakers to do their job. Government is designed to yield to the will of the majority. But this is not the way our current government operates. We now have a minority group running our country. The majority of citizens must bend to *their* will. Currently, our country is, at best, a charade of a democracy.

You and I, the voters, have enabled this agenda through the politicians we have elected. Look at the results of our actions or inactions. We have empowered those who are the very embodiment of the seven deadly sins. Daily we see the lust, gluttony, greed, sloth, wrath, envy, and pride of politicians at work. Elected officials who pay for sex, bully people on social media, cheat on their spouse, dodged the draft, and desecrate veteran war heroes. We have empowered elected officials to disregard facts and fabricate lies to benefit their needs while feeding the uneducated with false hope. We have empowered a health care system that places profits above a person's wellbeing. We have empowered elected officials who systematically hijack the government and mold it to their specific ideology with approval from their corporate and wealthy donors. We have empowered politicians who use immigrants and minorities as scapegoats for problems caused by a government serving only the elite. And we have empowered business earnings to come before the welfare of the everyday citizen. Are you proud of what we have created? I'm not.

Our government is broken, and I think it is time you and I, the voters, take responsibility and fix what we have created. We need to require all politicians to meet minimum ethical standards and conduct themselves in a highly professional manner. They must place the interest of the country's citizens above those of Big Money donors and lobbyists. We, the people, must come first. It is up to you and me, America's voters, to make this happen.

Our lives today are busy with many time constraints. Researching political candidates and issues is not a priority for most people. While we understand the need to vote, we often don't put in the necessary work to educate ourselves before casting our ballet. For some, the fallback option is to vote for one party. In my judgment, this is ill-informed voting and a significant cause of our country's division. Blind obedience to one party disregards the true characteristics and beliefs of a candidate. Scrutinizing a candidate politically and personally should be our top priority. Their traits and convictions must align with yours. After all, elected officials make decisions that affect both you and your family. Voting is a serious matter because you are giving politicians the power to control your life.

1. Traits I Require In A Politician

All too often, voters use irrational feelings to form a facade of a candidate. Mainstream media, party affiliation, social media, and friends are some sources we use to build this false image. Our illusion of a candidate obscures the real person and will not let the truth penetrate. Facts not fitting our perception are pushed away and dismissed. Rarely do we take time to see the genuine individual hidden by our mental guise. As a voter, I want to see behind the facade. I want to know and judge the candidates based on their traits.

Below, I list my required traits for politicians. While these may seem obvious to most, it is also apparent that voters are not demanding elected representatives meet minimum character standards.

From 2001 to present, 21 members of congress (13 Republicans and 8 Democrats), were convicted of a crime. Here are a few of their crimes: money laundering, bribery, felony tax evasion, lewd conduct, lying to law enforcement, possession of cocaine, sexual misconduct with a minor, racketeering, fraud, and insider trading.

One of these politicians was charged with bribery and then re-elected. Later he was convicted and removed from office. The fact that this person was re-elected after being charged with a crime should be as alarming to you as it is to me. As voters, it appears we have no character standards concerning the people we empower over us; accepting leaders and lawmakers that we would not have as friends. Why do we belittle ourselves In this way? Don't we deserve better?

By definition traits are distinguishing qualities of a person. They may be positive or negative qualities such as honesty versus deceit, or admiration versus contempt. The following are eight necessary traits a candidate must possess to earn my vote and meet my expectations of a true leader.

Honesty

First, I want honesty. Honesty should be an inherent personal quality in any candidate or elected official. So much so, that this requirement should not even be necessary to list. However, given the number of top government officials, both elected and appointed, connected to illegal or unethical acts, honesty doesn't appear to be a required quality by voters for political leaders. As a voter, I will assess a candidate's qualification based on their record of lying, cheating, or the use of political office for personal gain.

Respect

Respect everyone regardless of sex, sexual orientation, race, religious belief, country of origin, or political views. How hard is this concept? Every candidate, politician, or elected official must believe in this doctrine and act accordingly. Treat everyone the same and give equal opportunity to all. Politicians and appointed officials who vengefully denigrate people because of opposing viewpoints, the color of their skin, or choice of lifestyle, are not leaders; they are bullies. Bullies have no place in leadership. To earn my vote, candidates must listen to reasonable opinions, both agreeable and disagreeable. They willingly should debate issues and make the best decisions for the betterment of the people, the country, and the world

Integrity

The morality of any person running for an elected position should be held to the highest standard. People who cheat on their spouses, taxes, business relationships, or who bend the law to their favor, have proven they are untrustworthy and without integrity. This low moral, self-centered, egotistical person cannot be trusted to protect our democracy, the people of this country, and our place in the world. To win my vote, a politician must have the highest ethics, honor, and moral qualities achievable.

Knowledgeable

A deep understanding of historical and current events, combined with an awareness of political and physical geography, is essential for any politician to qualify for office. Without such knowledge, the mistakes of the past will be repeated. To truly change the future for the better, any endeavor undertaken to enact new policies and resolutions must be based on a complete comprehension of past and present events. I will vote for knowledgeable politicians that understand history and are willing to learn from it.

Rational and Diligent

Decisions that affect individuals, a country, or the world, must be based upon a deep understanding of facts and the surrounding issues. A thorough and exhaustive review of events and issues must be made before drawing a conclusion and moving forward. When the decision-making process is based on "gut feel", it does not utilize thoroughness and hard work to arrive at the best conclusion. Arriving at a conclusion first and then making the facts fit the decision is a manipulative distortion of the process. Choices made by gut feel and process distortion, are doomed to failure and driven by laziness, or the inability to understand the depth of an issue, or corruption, or all of these factors. Decisions made by politicians affect us as individuals either directly or indirectly. As such, a person's decision-making process is of paramount importance when evaluating their ability to hold elected office. Candidates who are diligent and arrive at rational decisions based on independently derived facts, have my vote.

Experience

We all dream and crave the "shining knight" politician who sweeps in from nowhere and makes the world a better place overnight. Somehow, we hold the belief that an outsider will make it all better. But before the light reflecting off the armor blinds us, we should consider the experience behind their suit of tin. It is easy for a candidate to make promises and spout rhetoric when they have limited understanding of the issues. The experienced politician knows the obstacles ahead and factors them accordingly. If a politician's armor is dinged up and tarnished with the scars of experience, this person is more likely to tell you the truth, even if it is not what you want to hear. My point is, we are all dreamers, but don't be so naive as to believe in fantasies. My vote is for the experienced candidate with proven results that benefit people, our country, and the world.

Disciplined

A disciplined person possesses strong self-control, achieves their goals, and has the mental toughness to withstand ridicule. These qualities give rise to an individual with good self-esteem who has an even temper and takes responsibility for their actions. An elected official that causes chaos and disparages others with differing opinions, lacks the discipline required to be a politician in a democracy. Low self-esteem candidates that blame and take vengeance on others who criticize them, lack discipline. I will not vote for them.

Vision

Elected officials and political leaders that strive to maintain the status quo as "good enough" are not leaders. They lack vision, courage, and the understanding of humankind's need to create, move forward, and build a better world. Leaders who are maintainers create a stagnant society with high levels of frustration. Any candidate or elected official should have a future vision that encompasses optimism, realism, and reaches past our current limits. They should be able to articulate their vision with passion and be passionate about achieving that vision. Most notably, the visions and achievements that made the United States a stronger, better nation happened almost 50 years ago. Sending a man to the moon, civil rights legislation, and environmental protection regulations were all visions that created a forward movement for our country. Since then, America has wallowed in the mud and stumbled backwards. I will vote for politicians with positive visions that reach to the edge of impossible.

2. Convictions I Require In A Politician

A person's convictions are the basis on which they take actions and achieve accomplishments. It is their belief system used to guide decision-making. A politician's convictions in a democratic government need to reflect the majority of the voter's viewpoint. Actions taken by legislators must be for the betterment of most citizens.

However, in our current government, the minority is winning favorable legislation over the majority's demands. Current polls show approximately 70% of Americans want a ban on the sale and ownership of assault weapons. Yet congress takes no action. Over 60% of voters want a tax increase on the wealthy. Again, no action is taken by congress. Most citizens desire Medicare for all. The political action taken is opposite of the American public's desires. Funding for the Affordable Care Act, a step toward Medicare for all, has been reduced and the act nearly gutted.

A group of politicians, backed by special interest organizations, have taken strategic positions within congress, enabling them to block reforms required by the majority of voters. Their convictions are self-serving and not aligned with the best interest of their constituents or the nation. I want politicians with the same convictions as mine, who will take action to bring about necessary change for the betterment of all.

Big Money Corrupts Politics

We are all aware that in today's politics, money equals influence. Candidates, primaries, elections, and legislation are all influenced by money contributed through various channels. For the most part, these channels are the domain of wealthy individuals, corporations, and special interest groups, i.e., "Big Money". The influence these individuals and organizations have over our political system skews the benefits of government to their favor. Such a one-sided influence is detrimental to the country and its citizens. The deranged belief that more corporate profits equal a better life for the average citizen is one example of the unbalanced influence in our political system. Removal of Big Money from politics will allow the voice of the majority, the average person, to be heard and acted upon. Elected officials must work for the betterment of all people. This belief can only be accomplished with the election of candidates who posses the conviction to remove Big Money from our political system.

Why is our political system so unbalanced? In January 2010, the Supreme Court issued a ruling in the Citizens United case that stated corporations could not be limited in making independent expenditures on elections. The ruling was based on the constitutional right of free speech. Before this decision, the right of free speech was restricted to an individual. Now it was being extended to include corporations, in the arena of politics. By broadening the scope of free speech, the court unleashed the enormous spending power of corporations onto politics. In other words, unlimited amounts of money can be spent in elections by corporations as long as they do not coordinate their spending with a candidate or political party.

Additionally, in March 2010, the D.C. District, U.S. Court of Appeals issued a decision, based on the January Supreme Court ruling, which enables unlimited contributions to independent expenditure groups. These court decisions have given rise to the Super PACs and "Social Welfare" nonprofit groups we see today. Through these organizations, wealthy individuals, corporations, and special interest groups can give unlimited amounts of money towards an election with the intention of influencing the outcome. Further, the rulings have opened the gates to allow foreign nationals, foreign corporations, and foreign governments to contribute large sums of money, the purpose being to sway our elections. Foreign money can flow through a Super PAC, as a US corporation owned by foreigners, or through social welfare organizations in the form of untraceable contributions. The nonprofit status of social welfare organizations allows donor names to be hidden from the public, thus giving rise to the term "Dark Money". This anonymous donor status provides the perfect cover for nefarious groups seeking to influence our elections.

Social welfare nonprofits and Super PACs often use their money to produce negative ads designed to control your vote. Typically, these ads have no basis in facts. Frequently, the ads are outright libel. Because groups paying for the advertisements are not officially associated with any candidate or political party, the ads are considered free speech. The commercial you see on TV, the sponsored post on Facebook, or the mailer you receive a few days before the election claiming candidate so-and-so to be a baby killer, was probably financed by a special interest group or foreign government seeking to change your vote and get their preferred candidate elected. The advertisement, which is strictly prohibited from endorsing a candidate, may not say which candidate they want you to vote for, but it will be strongly implied. So strong is the implication, the ad probably would not pass the independent expenditure test set by the courts and which should be enforced by the FEC (Federal Election Committee). But Big Money has effectively blocked the FEC from doing its job of enforcing election campaign finance regulations.

Why isn't the FEC enforcing regulations and controlling political spending? The FEC is mired in an ideological fight. Half of the committee is supporting Big Money. These FEC members believe campaign money, no matter where it comes from or the strings attached, should not be limited nor should their sources be exposed. It should be noted, politicians backed by Big Money placed these committee members on the FEC. The other half of the committee is trying to slow the flow of money, or at least identify the donors allowing us to determine the source of funding and who is pulling the strings. With the FEC split 50/50, it is at a stalemate, and campaign finance enforcement is at a standstill. The impotent committee enables Super PACs and Dark

Money organizations to receive and use large, unchecked amounts of money to influence our elections. In theory, Super PACs must report their donor's names and cannot accept donations from foreign sources. However, foreign-owned US corporations are donating to Super PACs with impunity. Here you see the FEC stalemate at work since half of the committee is unwilling to agree on what constitutes foreign ownership of a US corporation. Sources of Dark Money go completely unchecked as neither the FEC nor the IRS are sanctioned to address this problem.

The Supreme Court's Citizens United ruling opened the floodgates, allowing unlimited money to be spent on elections. When this ruling is combined with strategic control of the FEC, Big Money has successfully removed all campaign contribution restrictions, thereby enabling them to reshape the political landscape in their favor. This successful control strategy has turned campaign finance into the lawless Wild West with no sheriff in sight or one on the way.

What does this all mean? Basically, Big Money has bought and is buying elections, and doing it with impunity. This needs to be stopped.

Controlling the flow of money in elections is possible. It will take voter determination to make it happen. The most elegant solution to keep unchecked money out of politics is a constitutional amendment authorizing Congress to enact legislation for campaign finance controls. This is the most direct answer, but the process by which a constitutional amendment is brought into law, takes a long time and requires the strong will of the people to pass.

Additionally, congress could use tax legislation to close the wealth gap. Such tax regulations need to address both wealthy individuals and corporations since political money can flow from either direction.

Any such plan would need to be rigorously examined to eliminate loopholes and achieve the goal it was meant to accomplish.

In the near term, members of the FEC that block the committee's functionality need to be removed. The IRS must be allowed to enforce political donation restrictions on nonprofit organizations. While these near term fixes won't eliminate Big Money's influence on the system, they will at least put a sheriff in the territory.

Whatever the approach, it will take support by you and me, the voters, to change the situation. We must learn the truth and vote out politicians backed by Big Money in order to restore government for the people. This is not an easy task, but it can be done. Big Money only works if we allow it to influence the truth.

Climate Change Is Human Made

Climate change is, by far, the biggest crisis in our world today. It is a threat to our way of life and to humanity itself. The scientific evidence that climate change is human-caused is irrefutable. We cannot ignore this fact. People who deny climate change and its human causes are either greedy or stupid. We must not let greed and stupidity control our country and the world. The majority of the population believes in human-caused climate change, but yet our government does nothing. We all know greed is at the core of their inaction. I will only vote for politicians who believe in human-made climate change and who will take action to mitigate the causes.

As far back as the late 1800s, a Swedish scientist predicted the burning of fossil fuels would release

CO2 into the atmosphere and adversely affect our planet. Today we see these effects first hand. The burning of fossil fuels has driven atmospheric CO2 to its highest level in over 800,000 years. The greenhouse effect caused by the presence of atmospheric CO2, has resulted in our planet heating to levels never before seen by humans. The years 2015, 2016, 2017, 2018, and 2019, have been the hottest five years ever recorded. In 2018, 14 separate climate-related disasters caused over a billion dollars each in damage. In total, these 14 events cost governments and the world's population over $90 billion. Guess who is paying for these climate-related disasters? That's right, you and I pay in the form of higher insurance premiums, increased cost of goods, and higher taxes.

Disasters are not the only climate-related change affected by our planet's warming. Weather patterns are becoming less dependable. Seasonal changes that farmers have relied on for thousands of years to signal the planting and harvesting of crops are becoming unpredictable. Drought and flooding, coupled with increased pest and disease problems, are now affecting crop production. In the past, instances of crop failure were confined to a region. While devastating for that area, world food production could replenish food stocks for the stricken region. During the 1930's dust bowl, the Southern Plains of the United States experienced near 100% crop failure. However, crop production continued in the Northern Plains, the East, the South, and California. While the dust bowl lasted a decade, it had no real effect on food supplies throughout the country. Isolated crop failures do not pose a real threat to humankind. However, multiple large-scale crop failures do pose a threat. As we are now seeing, a rapidly changing climate opens the door for these failure events to occur in the form of drought, floods, pests, or diseases either by themselves or in combination with one another. This situation is much more serious than past isolated failures and will probably trigger a chain of events that include regional economic collapse, starvation, and mass migration, with the result being war.

But a warming planet is good news for some creatures such as mosquitoes, ticks, and other pests. Higher temperatures extend the habitat of disease-carrying mosquitoes to include the entire US mainland, enabling diseases such as Zika, dengue, and malaria to infect vast areas of the country. Disease-infected pests once restricted to tropical regions, will now ride the warming trend northward, right to your backyard. If it seems like I am making light of this, trust me, I am not. However, even today as we see Zika increase in Florida and move northward, the alarm has not been sounded to take action. Citizens are not demanding change on the part of politicians they elect. Does this indicate a complacent attitude by the majority of our population toward the effects of climate change?

As the planet warms, our oceans increase in temperature and, at the same time, becomes more acidic due to CO2 absorption. The warming, more acidic water kills marine life. Sea creatures with little or no mobility, such as coral reefs and shellfish, are the first to die off. Warmer seawaters also facilitate large-area algae blooms that reduce oxygen levels within regions of water, causing dead zones for fish and sea life. As you can see, climate change is not just about the surface landmass we live on. It affects the ocean, as well. Our seas have long been a food source for a large portion of the world's population. 60% of people in the world live within 60 miles of a coastline and depend on seafood for 15% of their protein intake. Look at this in a different way. The protein source for three meals per week comes from the ocean for 60% of the world's population. As the ocean warms and acidifies, coastal fisheries are at risk of dying out, increasing the risk of malnutrition and famine. This poses yet another threat to global stability.

Famine, unstable weather, billion-dollar disasters, and diseases are not the only effects of climate change. Flooding of low-lying coastal areas due to sea-level rise from melting glaciers is another change brought on by a warming climate. Coastal cities like Miami, New Orleans, and New York are feeling the effects of rising ocean levels, as well as thousands of smaller towns along the coast. Despite local efforts to hold back the sea, flooding will displace hundreds of thousands of people while simultaneously wiping out property values.

The most important thing to remember about climate change is that our planet's climate is interdependent. As the climate changes, it generates a butterfly effect around the world. For example, a small increase in ocean temperature can change seasonal rain patterns, increase hurricane strength, and reduce arctic ice. These complex changes can be difficult for the average person to understand. Industries that gain from the continued burning of fossil fuels use climate change complexity to sow the seeds of doubt regarding its reality.

Those who oversee fossil fuel companies are not deniers of climate change or the cause. Rather, they promote misleading information and buy political favors to support their fossil-fuel-burning scheme, knowing climate change has and will bring extraordinary transformation and destruction to our planet. Why do they deliberately enable climate change? The simple answer is to make more money. Every day that oil-producing companies are able to delay action on reducing fossil fuel burning, they sell $6.5 billion of oil. Fossil fuel's "deceive, drill, and burn" business model has served the oil and gas sector well. Money has always bought whatever the oil industry needed or wanted, including politicians.

The belief that wealth will and can guarantee personal survival feeds the greed of people in the fossil fuel profession. Money has always insulated the prosperous from society's problems, disasters, and prosecution for wrongdoing. In our world of greed and selfishness, the accumulation of wealth has always won. To the executives of fossil fuel companies, climate change is a nuisance, but not life-ending. They lack empathy for the strife climate change causes the average person.

The big question is not if climate change and the tragic events discussed above are going to occur, but how quickly they will happen? If the shift progresses slowly, most humans and animals will keep pace with a changing climate (assuming the changes do not make the planet uninhabitable). Impoverished and underdeveloped countries will be left on their own to find solutions for climate-triggered problems; problems they will be unable to solve unless they receive outside help. Displaced populations will bring about mass migration. People will die due to rising sea levels, famine, disasters, and diseases. A slower climate change means that the bulk of these tragedies will take place over the next few decades. When news of these events reach us our reaction, if history has taught us anything, will undoubtedly be the same as that of a school shooting. Do nothing. We know the reasons and how to stop these tragic events. But we turn our backs, become numb and complacent to the plight of others, even if it is our very own future playing out before our eyes.

If abrupt climate change happens, then it becomes a real threat to humanity. We will not adjust to the changes quickly enough, and the worst scenarios for humans will play out. Climate-related events will cause breakdowns in government and the possible collapse of civilization. I am not trying to be an alarmist, rather I am presenting a situation that could occur. To anyone who has study climate change, this scenario must be taken seriously. As a matter-of-fact, abrupt climate change is now the more likely situation because feedback loops are occurring as a result of the planet warming.

What is a feedback loop? As the planet warms, tundra frozen for thousands, if not millions, of years begins to thaw, releasing trapped methane into the air. Methane is a significantly more potent greenhouse gas than CO2. With increasing levels of methane released into the atmosphere, a warmer planet is created. The warmer climate thaws more tundra, this in turn releases more methane that increases the temperature which thaws more tundra that releases more methane. This cycle is a feedback loop.

The decrease in arctic ice and snow is creating another feedback loop. White or light colored surfaces, such as ice and snow, reflect the sun's radiation back into space. This reflective process dramatically reduces heat absorbed by the earth's surface, creating what is known as the albedo effect. As arctic ice and snow melt, the albedo effect decreases. Less polar ice and snow means the ocean and land absorb more heat. When more heat is absorbed, less ice and snow build up during winter months. With less snowpack and ice, there is more time for land and water to absorb the sun's heat. Thus, the loss of arctic ice and snow are creating another feedback loop.

Planet-warming feedback loops accelerate the planet's heating. Once started, they are difficult to stop. Stopping feedback loops requires significant cooling of the planet. Such cooling would require greenhouse gases to be lowered below preindustrial levels.

This is a slippery slope we have started down, and recovery may be near impossible. But here again, people who control the fossil fuel business know this. So why would they ignore well-documented facts? For the same reason people smoke cigarettes when they know they cause cancer. Instant gratification outweighs the risks. The gratification comes daily for oil companies in the form of $6.5 billion, enough to deny science and willingly turn a blind eye to the future. For the most part, we humans are greedy animals. We are smart enough to predict the future, but ignorant enough to gorge ourselves on the present when it suits us. Right now, it suits some politicians to gorge themselves on fossil fuel money at the expense of everyone's future.

I feel strongly about climate change and its affect on the future of our children and grandchildren. It frustrates and astonishes me to hear someone dismiss climate change as "just weather" and in the next sentence, say how much they love their family. If you really love your children and their descendants, wouldn't you be concerned about the world you are leaving them? This laissez-faire attitude fits with the inability to accept responsibility for our climate crisis. Just remember, your grandchildren are going to look back one day and ask why didn't grandma and grandpa do something to stop this from happening? They will look at your photo and wonder why you were so gullible to believe blatant rhetoric fueled by greed? To your grandchildren, your image will represent disappointment.

What can be done? Well, let's be real here. No one is going to give up burning fossil fuels overnight. We will not wake up tomorrow and see everyone driving an electric car powered by energy produced solely via wind or solar.

The good news is that today many of the products we need to start significant mitigation of climate change already exist. Electric production from wind and solar combined with energy storage technologies are currently in use. However, their use needs to be expanded and mandated with aggressive timelines. Fuel economy standards for vehicles need to be tightened to incentivize hybrid cars along with all-electric vehicles. In essence, it may be too late to stop climate change but not too late to mitigate

some of the most extreme effects by using our
current technologies or others currently in
development.

All is not lost if fossil fuel companies are kept out of
the political decision-making process. Oil-producing
tax subsidies must be removed, and oil companies
must be made to pay for their environmental
assassination. Only through the will of the voters by
electing the non-oil candidates and removing fossil
fuel money from politics can this be accomplished
within the time required to slow and stop the effects
of climate change.

Health Care Is A Right

Is your life worth less than mine? Is my life worth less than yours? Our current health care system places a value on our lives. Are not all lives of equal value? The health care system says no. The value of your life is directly related to the size of your bank account. This means health care is not a right but a privilege that can be bought. Is this humane? Is this fair for all? We must have politicians that embrace the belief of life over profit.

But isn't US health care the best in the world? Is this belief perpetuated by the AMA (American Medical Association), pharmaceutical and health insurance companies, hospitals, and some politicians a myth? Out of 21 developed nations, the United States ranked 20th for life expectancy and had the highest infant mortality rate. These results are not what should be expected of a country with a top-notch health care system. But there is one ranking where the US tops all other nations in health care, the amount we pay. Of the 21 developed nations, for 2017 the cost per capita in the United States was $10,209. The average cost per capita of other nations is about half that of the US at $5,290. That's right, we pay twice as much for an average shorter life expectancy and a higher infant mortality rate. So the belief appears to be a myth driven to achieve monetary gain for the health care industry.

The industry will debate life expectancy and infant mortality rates by saying those that receive health care live longer and have a lower rate of infant mortality. They are right. But because treatment and care within the system are based upon personal wealth, there is a large disparity in who has access to health care and who does not. In other words, the health care industry is saying: your life or the life of your baby is not worth as much as someone who has the means to pay. If you can pay, you live. If not, you die. Is this a fair system or a system driven by greed?

What is interesting about the health care debate is how the major political parties line up. On one side, you have the Democrats who, and I am generalizing here, are for health care for all and pro-choice on abortion. On the opposite side, you have the Republicans who want health care only for those that can afford to pay and they oppose abortion. It would seem that the issue of a high infant mortality rate would bring the two sides together. No matter which side of the abortion issue you are on, wouldn't it be beneficial for everyone to have the lowest infant mortality rate possible? The US has about six infant deaths per 1,000 births, while the average of the 21 developed nations is about 3 deaths per 1,000 births. At current birth rates, approximately 12,000 babies in the US could be saved each year with better health care access.

It is hard for me to understand the Republican stance on health care when I see them supporting and passing anti-abortion laws. They proclaim all life is sacred and must be protected. Then they offer the confusing view that health care is a privilege only for those who can afford it, thereby supporting a for-profit based health care industry. Is this the very definition of hypocrisy, or just good politics at work, or both? Politicians who use emotional ties connected to abortion and the pro-life platform in their quest to gain votes, are likely to be the same person turning a blind eye to high infant mortality rates caused by the current health care system they support. If you genuinely believe all life is sacred, then affordable universal health care for everyone should be a top priority along with or above anti-abortion legislation. But if you believe money is sacred and should be a major deciding factor determining who lives and who dies, then affordable health care is not a priority. So which is sacred, money or life? I think we see the answer in the needless deaths of 12,000 babies annually.

How did we get to a health care system designed for only those who can pay? To understand the US health care industry and how it has become what it is, we need to look at history. As we know it today, the health care industry began in the early 1900s with the introduction of health insurance. Through the first half of the twentieth century, health insurance was primarily offered by employers as a benefit to attract and retain employees. In the 1960s, health care costs started to increase. The reason for this is unclear. One source stated the cause for increased costs was due to more demand for health insurance. This makes sense on the surface, but insurance premiums should decline as the risk is spread over more people.

In 1960, a person spent an approximate average of 6.5% of their income on health care. During this time patients paid the majority of health-related expenses, with less than 25% being paid by health insurance companies. By 2013, health care cost had increased to just over 22% of a person's income. This trend of increasing cost began in the 1960s and continues to this day. These statistics confirm what you already know. Today, health care is a significant personal expense, and as history has shown, it will become more expensive over time if action is not taken to stop this upward escalation.

During the 1930s, the government discussed a national health insurance program. It never materialized due to opposition from the AMA. Subsequent attempts to establish universal health care within the country have all been halted through successful lobbying efforts by the health care industry. Not only has lobbying actions stopped health care reform, they have also succeeded in ending legislation for price controls on drugs, medical procedures, and diagnostic testing, to name a few examples. All of these cost-controlling measures, from basic health care to the most advanced medical procedure, exist in all developed countries except the US.

If history has shown us anything, it is that the idea of a "free market" working to lower prices does not apply to the current health care industry structure. Why? When was the last time you shopped for health care? I am not talking about insurance but rather the actual treatment or cure you needed. My guess is never. If you attempted to access specific costs for a medical procedure, the system offers you nothing in the way of information or pricing. In our current health care system, you are not the customer, you are only the patient.

The health care industry is unique in that its business transactions involve three parties with different goals: the patient, medical care provider, and health insurance company. The patient wants to be cured.

The medical care providers have the skills and tools to heal, plus they need to make a living from their services. Health insurance companies control the purse strings by collecting money from its customers, the patients, and making payments to medical care providers. The health insurance companies decide on the treatment you will receive, if any, based on the procedure's cost. While you can pay for treatment out-of-pocket if you so choose, most treatment costs are too expensive for the average person to afford without help from insurance providers. This leaves the health insurance companies as the primary health care decision-makers and the primary source of revenue for the medical care providers. In the classic sense, a customer is someone who pays for services or goods. Thus, in health care, the health insurance companies are the customers of the medical care providers, not the patient. This gives the health insurance companies great leverage within the industry and control over the patient's health. Insurance companies are not in business to treat you or make you healthy. They are in business to make a profit. The three parties involved in the health care process do not have a common goal. This is the inherent flaw of our current health care system.

As health insurance payments played a more significant role in health care, the health care industry evolved to be insurance-centric and not patient-centric. Obviously, this system does not provide the best solution for the patient, as it is designed to provide the highest profit for insurance providers.

Because health insurance has became a substantial part of the health care equation, more requirements are now placed on medical care providers to obtain payments from health insurance companies. These requests place a financial burden on the providers. In turn, medical care providers need to increase prices to cover the cost of insurance reporting. While it may seem that I am targeting the health insurance industry as the cause of our expensive health care system, I want to point out that medical care groups (i.e., doctor groups), hospitals, pharmaceutical companies, medical device manufacturers, malpractice insurance providers, nursing homes, and all other organizations associated with the health care industry, are also making a profit. No wonder the cost of our privately run health care system has grown unchecked, like a malignant tumor.

Understand that we, you and I, have fed the tumor and enabled its growth. Not with the money we feed it, but rather by electing politicians that allow health care and special interest groups to influence regulations. Uninformed and misinformed voters have enabled the current system by believing the health industry's strategic campaign of misinformation used to promote the current wealth-based system. Their tactics turn health care into an emotional issue with irrational arguments. In the past, the tobacco industry successfully used this approach, and the fossil fuel industry is currently using this same tactic. As we have seen, this strategy works on those unfamiliar with facts. Health care industry money is often used towards media ads and social media content with the intent of influencing voters to support the current for-profit system. They use emotional and irrational arguments designed to discredit a universal, single-payer health system by using terms like socialized medicine, government-controlled, increased taxes, job loss, and descriptions of patients having to wait for treatment or prescription medicine. In contrast, countries with universal single-payer health care overseen by the government have higher life expectancies, lower infant mortality rates, and less personal stress about paying for health care.

If you believe life is sacred, you must believe in universal, single-payer health care for all. If you believe health care is a right of every citizen, then you must believe in universal, single-payer health care for all. As voters, we need to vet political candidates and current elected officials to determine their conviction in moving towards a universal, single-payer health care system and bring positive change for all.

Clean Air And Water Must Be Preserved

How did the EPA (Environmental Protection Agency) become the villain? The government agency charged with protecting our air and water has been portrayed as a job-stealing villain. Why? This villainization strategy has allowed special interest groups and industries, with the help of key politicians, to continuously peck away at the EPA organization and regulations. A weak EPA enables industries to pollute more at the expense of public health. Why have we, the voters, allowed this to happen? Isn't clean air and clean water good for all of us? A clean environment provides a healthier habitat, which means healthier people. Here again, we see profits before people. We must have politicians that embrace and believe in a clean environment regulated by a strong, well-staffed, and well-funded EPA.

How quickly we forget. Imagine these two scenarios: in Ohio, the Cuyahoga River is on fire; and in Pennsylvania, 20 people are killed by air pollution. Both events actually happened.

The Cuyahoga River frequently caught fire and burned due to pollution dumped in its waters. As early as 1868, the river would catch fire. During the next century, the Cuyahoga burned at least 13 times. By 1969, fire catapulted the burning river into national headlines, where it became the catalyst for the Clean Water Act of 1972. For those not familiar with northeast Ohio geography, the Cuyahoga River flows through Cleveland and discharges into Lake Erie. The polluted river contributed to Lake Erie becoming the most contaminated great lake in the country prior to the enactment of the Clean Water Act. After 1972, it was illegal for industries to pollute waterways, watersheds, and water resource systems. So successful were the regulations that less than 20 years after the passage of the Clean Water

Act, the Cuyahoga River and Lake Erie became a recreational waterway with a vibrant waterfront business district in Cleveland. The Cuyahoga River is just one example of many waterways that have been revived due to strong EPA regulations and enforcement.

In our second example, 20 people were killed in 1948 due to toxic air pollution emissions from zinc and steel processing plants in Donora, Pennsylvania. In the early part of the 20th century, steel mills were established in Donora, transforming the farming community located in a valley along the Monongahela River in Western Pennsylvania, into a hub of steel production. The mills, factories, and homes all burnt coal as a source of fuel and heat. Pollution produced from burning coal often filled the valley, leaving it hazy and smog-filled. In the 1920s, local farmers sued the zinc mill for damages to their crops and livestock inflicted by air pollution created by the factory. This appears to be the first air pollution lawsuit filed by citizens in the US against an industry. By 1948, when the Donora deaths occurred, the haze of air pollution had become a part of everyday life for area residents. On October 30th of that year, the first person died. Within two days, air pollution had killed a total of 20 people. Physicians who investigated the deaths estimate that thousands more had died prematurely due to lung cancer, fatal asthma attacks, cardiovascular disease, and a variety of other cancers, during prior decades when unregulated mills polluted the town's air.

Soon after the deadly event, the federal government was asked to investigate the 1948 Donora incident. Their findings were greatly influenced by the mills' economic dominance in the area. The investigation concluded that while the mills do emit fine heavy metal particles and poisonous gases into the air, an atmospheric temperature inversion that trapped a deadly gas mixture in the valley was the major factor for the fatalities. As you can see, this is a twisted conclusion akin to having a drunk driver hit you and then claim it was the car's fault. (As a side note, we see this same type of irrational reasoning around climate change by those unwilling to accept the facts, thereby ignore the consequences they carry.)

While tragic and preventable, the Donora deaths were the impetus needed to convene the first national air pollution conference in 1950. Thirteen years later in 1963, the first Clean Air Act was passed by Congress, leading the way for creation of the EPA in 1970.

By the end of the 1970s, our country led the world in pollution control technology as well as implementation for cleaning up water and air emissions produced by industry. The EPA spearheaded strong regulations, forcing polluters to install technology and comply with new environmental laws. Automotive companies regularly complained to Congress, or anyone that would listen, that current technology was not mature enough to move into production. The EPA pushed back. The results were more fuel-efficient vehicles and exhaust emissions lowered by over 95%. Power plants and other industries were forced to comply with emissions-curbing regulations by reducing or eliminating air and water pollution. Pesticides, herbicides, and fungicides all came under scrutiny by the EPA due to their contamination of the food we eat, the water we drink, and the environment where we live.

As a country, we were reducing our pollution and cleaning up our environment while other nations continued to shorten the lives of their citizens by allowing industrial activities to pollute air and water needed to sustain human life. Our country was leading by example, becoming the envy of the industrial world. By the 1980s, Japan, Australia, and some countries in Europe were following our lead. In their efforts to catch up, these industrial countries became importers of our technologies for pollution control and mitigation. To supply this demand for technology, a whole new industry, with a significant job base, grew in the US. By the middle of the 1980s, the United States was exporting almost a billion dollars worth of goods and services directly related to technologies developed here in our country. Indirectly, EPA regulations had created a foreign market for products manufactured in the US.

The EPA is designated as the ordinary person's enforcement for mitigating and eliminating pollution in our environment that adversely affects health. But industry perceived the agency as the enemy. The EPA told industry what they could and could not do. Corporate leaders use to making their own rules, found this troubling, setting the stage for a showdown. To fight back, corporations used the EPA as a scapegoat. Every time layoffs occurred or jobs were lost, companies blamed the EPA and its regulations for cutting into bottom-line profit, eroding industry's competitive edge. In reality, these jobs would have been lost anyway due to globalization. But by placing blame on the EPA, industry was turning the public protector into a perceived public enemy. Employees who lost their jobs, needed to place blame on someone. Companies gave them the target: the EPA and their regulations.

However, the real reason for job losses was the availability of cheap labor in developing countries. Yes, other countries did not have those pesky environmental regulations. Complying with EPA regulations was only a small expenditure off of the corporate bottom line. Wage expenses were the real cost they were trying to cut. It is hard for a corporation to resist a 60% to 80% reduction in direct labor expenses. All they needed to do was move product manufacturing offshore to realize savings. By claiming the cost to comply with EPA environmental regulations as the reason for moving jobs overseas, corporations were able to deflect the real reason for job loss and gain an ally against the EPA, in the blue-collar worker. The corporate strategy of misinformation and disinformation surrounding the EPA was working. The inconceivable was happening. Working people began blaming the EPA for the loss of their jobs.

The next step in the villainization process of the EPA was to recruit prominent people to repeat the blame and inaccuracies, thus beginning a systematic dismantling of the agency. Enter the politicians. It is no secret that during the 1980s, Republicans took up the corporate call to blame EPA regulations for job losses. By the late 1980s, emission standards were relaxed resulting in a general eroding of EPA status. This was accomplished through underfunding, understaffing, and reducing or removing regulations altogether, allowing industries to pollute without retribution. The agency became ineffective and the public took notice that the EPA was not doing its job. They were right. An underfunded and non-supported agency is powerless by design. As a result, the pollution control technology created by America, and American made, along with the jobs associated with this technology, dispersed to other countries. Today instead of being a net exporter, we are an importer of high-tech pollution control products. Jobs and revenues that were created by EPA technology-forcing regulations, are now lost forever.

Today, the villainization of the EPA is near complete. The last step is to denounce its scientists and reduce agency funding to the point where critical personnel leave. This step is now taking place under the current administration. Once the guiding star of the world, the EPA has now been reduced to a shell of its former self.

The water crisis of Flint, Michigan, is another example of underfunding enabling people to blame the EPA. For Flint residents, the agency was slow to act, endangering their lives. They were right. The agency was and is dysfunctional. It has become so politicized that employees fear retaliation if they speak the truth rather than use the correct political rhetoric when responding to an environmental or health-related event. With a reliable, efficient, and non-political EPA, the Flint water fiasco would have been exposed much sooner. Or possibly, it would have never happened.

Corporate America is slowly getting its way of profit over people. Soon the Cuyahoga River will again be on fire and polluted air will again kill. Don't worry, the corporations that poison our water and air will be happy to tell you its just a natural phenomenon. Everything is fine and under control.

Case in point, fracking. Fracking has been directly linked to earthquakes and groundwater pollution. But according to the oil and gas industries, there is no real evidence establishing fracking as the cause. Remember, with corporations in control, everything will be fine, "trust me," they say. With the EPA unable to do its job, there is no watchdog to protect the individual from unscrupulous industry practices. Unchecked fracking, which all fracking really is, is the perfect example of industry policing itself.

Corporations are right about who controls everything. They do. But remember it is you and I that gave them control through the politicians we voted into office. We, the people, can take back control and we must do exactly that.

We must resurrect the EPA and make it stronger than before. The agency must be protected from politicians who promote a pro-profit corporate agenda. The real purpose of the EPA is to protect us, the people of this country. This is accomplished by setting standards, implementing regulations, and policing industries to safeguard our health and protect the environment. Failure to do so moves us backward to 1940 and enables more Flint water crises to occur. We cannot let this happen.

68

Gun Regulations Are Essential

How does a country grow numb to children being shot and killed at school? How can a minority of people and special interest groups, like the NRA and gun manufacturers, hold a whole country hostage? Does a private citizen need a semi-automatic weapon? Or carry a gun with them at all times? The insanity associated with firearms and the lack of sensible laws is only surpassed by the reaction and inaction of key politicians after every mass shooting. Gun money flowing to many elected officials has parallelized gun regulation efforts, enabling gun manufacturers to profit at the expense of public safety and welfare. Politicians hide behind the 2nd amendment, using it as their shield. At the same time, they allow children and law-abiding citizens to become casualties in the war for gun profits. Touting personal safety and the "American way of life" by so-called pro-gun politicians, gun legislation has been transformed into an emotional argument rather than a rational issue requiring examination of the facts. In reality, guns take more lives than they save. Candidates and elected officials that I will vote for, must believe in strong gun regulations.

How did guns become the politically charged issue it is today? Gun rights advocacy groups such as the NRA have successfully convinced citizens into believing that for personal safety and to be a "real American", you must own a gun. They use TV news sensationalism coupled with social media know-it-alls to fuel their cause. Everytime a gun kills someone, pro-gun groups proclaim more guns are needed to stop the killings. Their response to a school shooting is to arm the teachers. Why? Because in their words, "guns save lives". Let's not forget this approach also promotes gun sales. In 2019, approximately $9.7 billion was spent in the US on guns and gun-related accessories. To put this into perspective, it is almost the same amount spent on new refrigerators during the same time period, which was $9.4 billion. This comparative statistic is both amazing and alarming at the same time. Who would have thought more money would be spent on a nonessential item such as a gun, versus a necessary appliance, a refrigerator? Have people been so brainwashed as to believe a gun is essential for living in this country?

America is the land-of-guns. As a nation, gun owners in the US possess enough guns to arm each man, woman, and child in the country with 1.19 guns per person. The next closest nations with the highest gun ownership per person are: Montenegro, Uruguay, Canada, Finland, and Iceland, with 0.3 firearms per person. In the United States the total number of firearms is approximately 390 million. Of those, about 15 to 20 million are semi-automatic weapons owned by civilians. These guns are designed with the expressed intent of killing people. For comparison, the US military has 4.5 million guns. In other words, there are four times more weapons designed and manufactured to kill people in the hands of civilians than in the hands of our military. Why? Are we so afraid of our neighbors or the people living in the next town that we must arm ourselves at a higher rate than the professional military protecting our country? Are we that paranoid?

FBI statistics show violent crime (murder, rape, robbery, and aggravated assault) in the US has been declining since the early 1990s and is now at the same rate per capita as 1970. Property crime, such as burglary and theft, is also down. Murder, a component of the violent crime statistics, is at the same per capita rate as the early 1960s. This is a positive trend. A gun owner or a pro-gun advocate could make the assumption from this information that increased gun ownership is decreasing the crime rate. But before you consider this a vindication for "more-guns-the-better" stance, let's compare violent crime statistics of similar countries to the US. By similar, I mean those with an equal standard of living and culture as ours.

The statistics I used are from the European Union (EU) for 2017. In 2017, the EU was composed of 28 independent nations unified by agreement to act as one group regarding trade and movement between the countries. Yes, I am simplifying the relationship between EU countries. Still, the borders separating these countries have virtually been eliminated, allowing people, guns, and crime to flow freely from nation to nation. This borderless group of nations is similar to the 50 states comprising the United States. Different EU countries have varying laws related to guns and gun ownership, just like the states of the US, but no one is stopping you at the border checking for guns. As a whole, the EU and the US can be considered developed nations. As of 2017, the EU's Gross Domestic Product (GDP) was $15 trillion, compare to the US at $19.5 trillion. Furthermore, the

EU and US cultures are closely linked because most Americans have European roots connecting many of our traditions and values.

As already stated, there are 1.19 guns per person in the US, with the next closest EU countries of Austria and Finland at 0.3 guns per person. The US has 394 million guns in civilian hands compared to the EU at 64 million. Thus, the US has six times as many guns owned by civilians as the EU. If you are a believer in "the more guns you have the safer you are" theory, than the US should be six times safer or at least somewhat safer then the EU.

The 2017 crime statistics data shows this is not the case. If you live in the EU, your chances of being killed or murdered by someone else is 1 in 119,000. If you live in the US, your chances of being murdered are 1 in 19,000. The US has six times the number of guns, and your likelihood of being murdered is six times greater. Coincidence? Maybe. But I don't think you can argue the apparent fact that increased availability of guns also increases the probability of someone using one. Imagine you and your neighbor become entangled in a disagreement. One person is so overcome by anger, that a firearm is used to settle the dispute. Or a road rage incident where one driver becomes so incensed that a gun is pulled. These events happen on a daily basis and turn deadly because a firearm was readily available. Fewer guns circulating in a nation, equals a safer society. Countries that have limited gun ownership through regulations are many times safer than our country.

I don't care if a mentally stable, nonviolent individual trained in gun safety, owns a gun for hunting. A single-shot, bolt-action rifle or pump-action shotgun should work just fine for killing any defenseless animal. A hunter does not need to use a semi-automatic weapon when hunting. Of course, most guns are not purchased for the purpose of hunting; they are purchased to kill people under the guise of self-protection. How do I defend myself and my family with a single-shot rifle or shotgun when the "bad guys" have much more powerful weapons? I need semi-automatic or even automatic guns for self-defense. Here we see the one-sided logic for owning bigger guns and stockpiling weapons. This circular argument is precisely what the gun interest groups want you to believe, escalating emotion while leaving reasoning behind. If personal safety is the goal, then the facts point directly to the restriction of gun ownership and the sale of semi-automatic weapons to the public.

In 2008, a Supreme Court ruling stipulated that the individual has the "right to bear arms". In 2010, the court ruled that state and local gun laws may not interfere with this right. However, the 2010 ruling was accompanied by a comment from Justice Alito, a conservative, stating, "the court did not mean to cast doubt on laws prohibiting possession of guns by felons and people who suffer from mental illness, laws forbidding carrying guns in sensitive places like schools and government buildings, or laws regulating the commercial sale of firearms." This comment appears to be a blueprint for gun regulation.

Federal legislation should be enacted to make it illegal for felons, and anyone convicted of a violent crime, including domestic violence, to own or possess a gun. This list should include people who are mentally ill, as well as no guns should be sold to anyone under the age of 30. All gun owners and users must be required to pass a government-operated training course. Limit the number of firearms possessed by any one person to two. Independent gun stores should be abolished with gun sales and training to take place only through federally operated facilities. The selling or transfer of firearms between private individuals must be made illegal. These actions would assure uniformity in gun availability, background checks, registration, and training while conforming to the Supreme Court's ruling.

Whatever approach is used, it is clear that guns need to be regulated. We need and must have candidates and elected officials that will pass strict gun regulations. Gun madness and obsession need to end if we are to advance as a society.

The Common Thread Of Manipulation

Throughout this section, you may have noticed the reoccurring theme of how Big Money has influenced our government. This should not surprise you given the Supreme Court rulings permitting unchecked money to be spent on elections. The inequitable distribution of wealth in America has given rise to the ultra-wealthy, those with over $100 million in net worth. A person with such financial strength is now free to become a force in government without being known or held accountable for their political actions.

You must credit the ultra-wealthy and corporate leaders (in other words, the oligarchs), because they have swayed the government and its policies to their favor. Through political influence they have lowered taxes on the rich, reduced business regulations, and cut funding for social programs and public schools.

The elite achieved these goals by using their enormous prosperity combined with the unlikeliest of allies, the unwitting average blue-collar worker. As a group, hourly paid workers incur more financial burden from a wealth-centric ideology promoted by politicians who are aligned with the elite. Through well-organized campaigns selling emotions rather than facts, hard working folks are manipulated into voting for candidates who support an agenda that is not in their personal best interest. It is hard to argue with the effectiveness of this tactic. Over time, it has placed wealth-backed, like-minded politicians in strategic areas within the government, enabling them as the controlling minority.

I use the term "controlling minority" because the oligarch-controlled politicians do not respond to the desires of most American citizens as is required in our democracy. The majority of people want legislation on stricter gun control (70% of voters); energy policies that reduce fossil fuel burning to mitigate climate change (67%); stronger protection of clean air and water (68%); Medicare for all (69%); and limits on campaign spending (77%). But no new laws are being considered on any of these issues. Why? Changes sought by the majority are against the controlling minority's stance of profit over people.

When legislation to address the above issues is proposed, the controlling minority labels the proposal as a social program, anti-American or anti-free market. They deflect the real concerns and demands of the people by creating an emotionally charged topic. The majority is no longer in control. Our country has slipped further away from democracy and is moving toward fascism.

See if you recognize this: a governing group that supports the suppression of opposing opinions; responds to events in a highly authoritarian and nationalistic way; and supports far-right views that include the white supremacy doctrine of blaming immigrants and minorities for every problem imaginable. Sound familiar? It should, taking into account current events. And it should scare you. This is fascism. We fought World War II to stop fascism. Now we are enabling it in our country by electing oligarch-backed candidates using the above philosophy to gather votes.

Today, these politicians are using their status and power to advance a form of wealth-centric fascism over the best interest of the working class and the nation. The agenda of "profits at any cost" is a thread that runs throughout this book. As a result, we see our democracy being change into a de facto government controlled by oligarchs for the benefit of wealthy.

Consider the "defund to fail" strategy used by politicians who want to hamstring a government agency's effectiveness. The approach slowly causes an organization to underperform, becoming dysfunctional through the gradual reduction of funding. After a prolonged period of underfunding, the agency does not meet the public's expectations. Politicians convince voters it is a failure. When the funding plug is finally pulled, few people care. This is a brilliant strategy used by politicians and their backers to get what they want, avoiding the annoying legislative process and accompanying bad press.

Government agencies and programs that benefit workers are a target of this strategy. Ironically, blue-collar workers who are the beneficiary of worker-advocate agencies are the voters that elect politicians who reduce funding for these very same groups. The "defund to fail" strategy has been and is being applied to the agencies of Occupational Safety and Health Administration (OSHA), Mine Safety and Health Administration (MSHA), and the National Institute for Occupational Safety and Health (NIOSH). These organizations are chartered with protecting workers by enforcing health and safety regulations in the workplace.

Many businesses believe the endeavors of the above agencies have a negative impact on profit. Seeking to minimize safety costs, companies turned to political channels to remove this alleged burden. The political solution is to implement the "defund to fail" strategy. This process began in the 1980s when agencies faced funding cuts, leading to staff decreases. In 1980, OSHA's enforcement section had a budget of $300 million, with 15 compliance inspectors per one million workers. By 2016, the budget decreased to $208 million, with the number of inspectors at 5 per one million workers. Subsequently from 2011 to 2018, there was a 12% increase in worker fatalities.

Government agencies designed to protect hard working citizens are being systematically underfunded to gut their effectiveness, with the goal being to abolishing them altogether. The blue-collar sector has enabled this strategy by voting for candidates who condemn "big government" as bad for the country, a PR slogan invoking an emotional reaction, causing a person to vote against their best interest. This is one example where voters need to look behind the hype and see the true motive of profit over people. A citizen allowing emotion to control their vote rather than reason, is being manipulated and made into a fool.

In Closing

Our democracy has been stolen. Today, we are ruled by a minority of politicians who are empowered and guided by special interest groups, corporations, and the ultra-wealthy. To gain votes, politicians use rhetoric designed to enlist an emotional response from ill-informed voters. Their vote-getting script includes blaming immigrants and minorities for our country's problems; promoting conspiracy theories about anyone who stands against them; attacking the press for presenting factual information that contradicts their lies; and spouting pro-gun and anti-abortion slogans. This bombastic approach is designed to stir emotions while being void of substance. Appealing to those who are uninformed on the issues. Producing proven results, this tactic has convinced enough citizens to vote against their personal best interests, thereby enabling a wealth-centric, fascist-like government.

The desires of the majority of Americans are being swept aside. Calls for action on campaign financing, climate change, clean air and water, health care, and gun control reform are going unanswered. What can be done?

Throughout this book, I have refrained from associating political parties to the actions I describe. I believe each candidate should be evaluated individually and not judged solely on party affiliation. However, when a group of politicians is acting as one, and their actions are opposite to the demands of the majority of the people, then it is time to name that group and treat them as one candidate. It has become evident to me, that Republicans are acting to advance the wealth-centric, fascist-like principles we see today in our government. The fact is, the majority of Americans do not support their opinions, position, or actions.

For future elections, I will not be voting for Republicans. Yes, this is going against what I state in this book about considering each candidate as an individual. But our country has strayed too far in one direction, being led by Republicans who are acting as a monolith. I cannot stand by and allow it to continue. I am voting Democratic to:

- Reclaim our democracy
- Restore civility to elected offices
- Remove hate from government
- Rebuild America's reputation as a world leader
- Take action on climate change
- Make health care a right for all
- Pass gun control laws
- Abolish the influence of Big Money from politics
- Reinvigorate agencies that protect the environment and worker's safety

The ideological battle to save our democracy can be won. To rid our government of current politicians who support wealth-centric, fascist-like philosophy, will take more than one election cycle. In the coming years, voters must remain vigilant and continue the quest for restoring our democracy.

I close with the last phrase from President Abraham Lincoln's Gettysburg Address. These words were spoken over 150 years ago when our country was at war with itself. Today, our resolve to be a democracy is being tested and Lincoln's words still ring true: *"that this nation, under God, shall have a new birth of freedom – and that government of the people, by the people, for the people, shall not perish from the earth"*.